END TIMES WOMAN:

PROVERBS 31 IN THE LAST DAYS

END TIMES WOMAN:

PROVERBS 31 IN THE LAST DAYS

A BIBLICAL WOMAN STUDY

D. A. FIEDLER

End Times Woman: Proverbs 31 in the Last Days

A Biblical Woman Study

Copyright © 2014 D. A. Fiedler

All scripture: The Holy Bible, King James Version. Underlining of scripture inserted by author.

Cover Image: Dreamstime

FOR JOY

ISBN-13: 978-1502331922

ISBN-10: 1502331926

E-Book ASIN: B00MO4R3UK

CONTENTS

Strength and honour are her clothing;
and she shall rejoice in time to come.
Proverbs 31:25

And when these things begin to come to pass,
then look up,
and lift up your heads;
for your redemption draweth nigh.
Luke 21:28

INTRODUCTION

Drawing wisdom from Proverbs 31 for the Last Days

The Christian woman of our age has witnessed changes in society at an accelerated rate. She lives in time where reestablished Israel is surrounded by enemies, and the love of many runs cold.

She may be single or married, head of household or keeping the household, raising children, or working outside the home.

She guards her faith, her home and her loved ones with all the heart of the Proverbs 31 woman, in an increasing fever pitch of broken down relationships and perilous times.

While the ideal world and resources of the Proverbs woman may seem like a distant dream to the woman of today, the truth and beauty of her life is in fact a strong parallel and source of encouragement.

The Lord warns us repeatedly to be wise and take heed, "indeed be as wise as serpents and meek as doves." With the climate ripe of the signs of the Last Days, don't our hearts cry out for wisdom on how to live?

Consider, for a moment, the book of wisdom as an example of the wise man. The creation for the woman or bride was saved for last. Just as God created woman last, after he created the world, man, Eden and all living creatures.

Her example, taken from the body of wisdom, given to us by God, is

beneficial for our hearts, homes and faith as time nears the end and biblical prophecy is being fulfilled.

This personal or group study covers the wisdom of Proverbs 31 in relation to the last days focusing on the attack on love, the attack on the home and the attack on faith.

- Faith: We are told repeatedly to watch and be ready, and we are encouraged by the blessings of overcoming. How can we keep a faithful, watchful walk with God?

- Love: We are forewarned of hardheartedness, the love of many growing cold, and the lukewarm church. How can we keep ourselves from this apathy which leads to apostasy?

- Home: We are warned that our homes will be under attack, family members will betray each other, as people will be lovers of self. Hardships will come against the home, the effects of the last days, deception, war, famine, the beginning of sorrows. How can we ready our homes for the days such as these?

Drawing wisdom from the Olivet discourse, Proverbs 31, biblical women, scriptures and comparing to current events, we find very real help on how to live forewarned in the time of sorrows.

ONE

DECEPTION & TRUST

And Jesus answered and said unto them,
Take heed that no man deceive you.
For many shall come in my name, saying, I am
Christ;
and shall deceive many.
Matthew 24:4-5

Who can find a virtuous woman? for her price is
far above rubies.
The heart of her husband doth safely trust in her,
so that he shall have no need of spoil. She will do
him good and not evil all the days of her life.
Proverbs 31:10-12

THE WARNING

The Lord first warns us to pay attention, to be mindful of the rise of deception and the attack on faith.

The pitfall of deception is a gaping abyss. Christians are constantly told we must be sensitive and inclusive to non-biblical theology. All the while, our faith, our Lord and His Holy word are demeaned.

THE WOMAN

Wisdom's call is to be a virtuous bride, a rare creature in evil times. A bride so faithful in love that her husband's heart is full of confidence.

A woman whose heart trusts in God and His Holy word, see's the world through spiritual eyes.

THE WISDOM

As the bride of Christ living in a politically correct age, Christian's are under constant attack to compromise their faith. A wise woman hears the voice of her Beloved and won't be so easily duped.

THE WORD

Let's read Paul's words on deception in regard to faith:

> *For I am jealous over you with godly jealousy: for I*
> *have espoused you to one husband, that I may*
> *present you as a chaste virgin to Christ. But I fear,*
> *lest by any means, as the serpent beguiled Eve*
> *through his subtilty, so your minds should be*
> *corrupted from the simplicity that is in Christ. For*
> *if he that cometh preacheth another Jesus, whom we*
> *have not preached, or if ye receive another spirit,*
> *which ye have not received, or another gospel, which*
> *ye have not accepted, ye might well bear with him.*
> *2 Corinthians 11:2-4*

The Lord instructs us to take heed, as He loves us and desires us to be ready for this time of deception.

> *For many deceivers are entered into the world, who*
> *confess not that Jesus Christ is come in the flesh.*
> *This is a deceiver and an antichrist.*
> *Look to yourselves, that we lose not those things*
> *which we have wrought, but that we receive a full*
> *reward.*
> *Whosoever transgresseth, and abideth not in the*
> *doctrine of Christ, hath not God. He that abideth*
> *in the doctrine of Christ, he hath both the Father*
> *and the Son.*
> *If there come any unto you, and bring not this*
> *doctrine, receive him not into your house, neither*
> *bid him God speed:*
> *For he that biddeth him God speed is partaker of his*
> *evil deeds.*
> *2 John 1:7-11*

The Bible tells us that a deceiver and antichrist is someone who does not preach the gospel according to the Bible, and even warns us not to invite them in.

When people who do not believe the word of God come proselytizing to your home, not letting them in has nothing to do with being religiously intolerant. It has to do with believing God's word and being faithful to Him.

Our witness of Christ's salvation cannot be stopped, it is beautiful, born of love, motivated and inspired by God and comes from the soul. We are clearly cautioned about agreeing only with the biblical truth of the gospel of Christ and of protecting the sanctity of our homes in very spiritually malicious days.

BIBLICAL WOMAN

Bible study: Eve

Reading: Genesis 1:26-31, Genesis 2-4

To consider:

A woman who was snuck up on by the father of lies.

> *Now the serpent was more subtil than any beast of*
> *the field which the LORD God had made. And he*
> *said unto the woman, Yea, hath God said, Ye shall*
> *not eat of every tree of the garden?*
> *Genesis 3:1*

Beautiful, beloved Eve walked in the garden with the Lord and yet Satan deceived her. We, born outside of Eden, who see through the glass dimly, must wholeheartedly trust in the truth of God's word in a day where it is constantly challenged.

As in the time of Eden where the serpent challenged, "...hath God said..?" we live in a time when everything is under debate, and the words of the enemy are an accepted mantra in all society.

Eve admitted to God that she had been deceived and then confessed that she ate the fruit.

> *And the LORD God said unto the woman, What is*
> *this that thou hast done? And the woman said, The*
> *serpent beguiled me, and I did eat.*
> *Genesis 3:13*

As wisdom's woman was not perfect, neither was Eve, nor are we. Eve was our first example on repentance and restoring faithfulness with God.

Being honest with God is the first step toward spiritual faithfulness. We all sin and fall short. We all need daily restoration.

MODERN WORLD

In our day, in the religion of Islam, they are currently seeking the arrival of their Islamic messiah figure whom they call Mahdi. He is said to be a 9th-century descendant of their prophet Mohammad whom the Shiites refer to as the 12th Imam.

We live in a day where many see godlessness as their salvation and as the salvation of society. They proselytize Atheism and preach against religion fiercely, ostracizing all whom they feel are religious and whom they consider weak.

We also live in a day where other religions declare they are Christian and claim to have the truth about Jesus. However their faiths do not rely on the Holy Bible, nor the gospel of Christ.

They discount the validity of the Bible aggressively, demean God's word and our Savior, yet then claim a badge of Christianity, as if for protection.

> *Heaven and earth shall pass away: but my words*
> *shall not pass away.*
> *Luke 21:33*

If you doubt God's word is reliable then I urge you to do a study on the meticulous transcription of His word over the centuries. The scriptures have undergone the highest scrutiny.1

He won't be offended if you seek the truth for yourself. God loves those who seek Him. So let's seek Him.

> *For I know the thoughts that I think toward you,*
> *saith the LORD, thoughts of peace, and not of evil,*
> *to give you an expected end.*
> *Then shall ye call upon me, and ye shall go and pray*
> *unto me, and I will hearken unto you.*
> *And ye shall seek me, and find me, when ye shall*
> *search for me with all your heart.*
> *Jeremiah 29: 11-13*

Seeking the Lord will give us understanding. Good judgment is needed during the days of deception.

> *Evil men understand not judgment: but they that*
> *seek the LORD understand all things.*
> *Proverbs 28:5*

Hold on tight to the Lord. Stay close to Him in prayer, let's let faith in the Lord and in His Word be on the top of our list of desired virtues.

TAKING IT TO HEART

Are we listening to people who are trying to dissect the validity of God's word, people who say the Bible cannot be trusted, is not accurate, and that we need their insight, guidance, literature, prophets opinion etc. to know the truth?

We are to fear God not man. (Matt 10:28) Let's close the door on those who echo the serpent, and have theories and doctrines from their own imaginations and uncircumcised hearts, for from their hearts their mouths speak. We, as believers, must cling to the heart of God and His Holy word.

Our choices, like Eve's, will affect not only our lives but also the lives of our family members.

It is very painful to be deceived, especially in regard to God. The only way to know His word is to read His word.

Draw nigh to God, and he will draw nigh to you.
James 4:8

PERSONAL APPLICATION

Knowing that the time is thick with deception, how can we prepare and walk in faithfulness? Let's take a moment to prayerfully apply God's word to our lives.

FAITH

What can you do to build/protect your faith during the days of deception?

Establish closeness with God.

Daily prayer: Let God in.

Read scripture: Really get to know Him.

Believe: His promises.

Praise Him: He is so good, let Him know.

Overcoming: Like Eve, we can restore our relationship with the Lord through confession of sin and turn back to the Lord in faith.

> *For as the heaven is high above the earth, so great is*
> *his mercy toward them that fear him. As far as the*
> *east is from the west, so far hath he removed our*
> *transgressions from us. Like as a father pitieth his*
> *children, so the LORD pitieth them that fear him.*
> *Psalms 103:11-13*

We can live lives faithful to the Lord.

List ways you are inspired to keep free from deception in regard to your faith.

LOVE

What can you do to build/protect your love during the days of deception?

Jesus says in the last days the attack on love comes in many ways, and that people will grow hardhearted. Protecting the hearts and love in our homes should be a top priority.

We can avert the deception of being clouded by offense and being unforgiving. We can restore strained relationships in our families, if at all possible, as soon as possible.

We can show our love, and walk in love, faithful to our household.

List ways you are inspired to keep free from deception in regard to your love.

HOME

What can you do to build/protect your home during the days of deception?

We can practice discernment over who or what we invite into our homes.

We can assess our household needs. The times are increasing in turmoil and we can prepare. The Lord warned us because He loves us.

Let's take stock of our pantries and homes and set forth a plan, seek the Lord and put faith in action.

Food storage basics: **Canning and dying foods** (See Appendix II)

First let's look to the words of Christ.

> *Therefore take no thought, saying, What shall we eat? or, What shall we drink? or, Wherewithal shall we be clothed?*
> *(For after all these things do the Gentiles seek:) for your heavenly Father knoweth that ye have need of all these things.*
> *But seek ye first the kingdom of God, and his righteousness; and all these things shall be added unto you.*
> *Take therefore no thought for the morrow: for the morrow shall take thought for the things of itself. Sufficient unto the day is the evil thereof.*
> *Matthew 6:31-34*

We are to remember not to fear, or worry as we look to our pantry needs, but to trust God. We fill our homes not in fear but in faith. The Lord knows our needs as keepers of the home, He will provide.

We can act in faith and prepare for the days of sorrows, watching and believing the Lord's warnings. To be found ready for His return, a faithful and good steward of what He has entrusted us.

List ways you are inspired to keep free from deception in regard to your home.

NOTES:

TWO

WAR & WISDOM

And ye shall hear of wars and rumours of wars:
see that ye be not troubled:
for all these things must come to pass,
but the end is not yet.
Matthew 24:6

She seeketh wool, and flax,
and worketh willingly with her hands.
She is like the merchants' ships;
she bringeth her food from afar.
She riseth also while it is yet night, and giveth
meat to her household,
and a portion to her maidens.
Proverbs 31:13-1

THE WARNING

The Lord's second warning is of intensifying events of war, but he comforts us to keep faith through it and understand it will happen before the end.

THE WOMAN

The woman of wisdom prepares her home for the events surrounding her life for the current day, and looks with wisdom for the needs of the future.

A woman who brings her food from afar goes to get a deal and an adequate supply. She takes care of her pantry, it is important to her.

THE WISDOM

A wise woman provides for the needs of her family members. Being forewarned of impending war, she will prepare to the best of her abilities.

THE WORD

Let's consider the Lord's words on the ruler over his household.

> *Therefore be ye also ready: for in such an hour as ye*
> *think not the Son of man cometh. Who then is a*
> *faithful and wise servant, whom his lord hath made*
> *ruler over his household, to give them meat in due*
> *season? Blessed is that servant, whom his lord when*
> *he cometh shall find so doing.*
> *Matthew 24:44*

A wise woman will provide sustenance, (nourishment for the body and soul), for her family members.

> *There is treasure to be desired and oil in the*
> *dwelling of the wise; but a foolish man spendeth it*
> *up.*
> *Proverbs 21:20*

The Lord says it is both faithful and wise, and says we will be blessed.

BIBLICAL WOMAN

Bible study: Abigail

Reading: I Samuel 25:2-42

To consider:

Abigail had been busy at home (working with wool), and was ready with provisions. She knew God's will for her day, and she protected her household. David was coming and she was ready, in both her home and her heart.

David sought sustenance for his men, his soldiers, who had been watching over Nabal's servants and livestock. Nabal responded rudely, and David sought justice.

> *But one of the young men told Abigail, Nabal's wife, saying, Behold, David sent messengers out of the wilderness to salute our master; and he railed on them.*
> *But the men were very good unto us, and we were not hurt, neither missed we any thing, as long as we were conversant with them, when we were in the fields:*
> *They were a wall unto us both by night and day, all the while we were with them keeping the sheep.*
> *Now therefore know and consider what thou wilt do; for evil is determined against our master, and against all his household: for he is such a son of Belial, that a man cannot speak to him.*
> *Then Abigail made haste, and took two hundred loaves, and two bottles of wine, and five sheep ready dressed, and five measures of parched corn, and an hundred clusters of raisins, and two hundred cakes of figs, and laid them on asses.*
> *1 Samuel 25:14-18*

She provided not only physical food but also nourishment for David's soul as well, in the form of a blessing.

> *Now therefore, my lord, as the LORD liveth, and as thy soul liveth, seeing the LORD hath withholden thee from coming to shed blood, and from avenging thyself with thine own hand, now let thine enemies, and they that seek evil to my lord, be as Nabal.*
> *And now this blessing which thine handmaid hath brought unto my lord, let it even be given unto the*

young men that follow my lord.
I pray thee, forgive the trespass of thine handmaid:
for the LORD will certainly make my lord a sure
house; because my lord fighteth the battles of the
LORD, and evil hath not been found in thee all thy
days.
Yet a man is risen to pursue thee, and to seek thy
soul: but the soul of my lord shall be bound in the
bundle of life with the LORD thy God; and the
souls of thine enemies, them shall he sling out, as out
of the middle of a sling.
And it shall come to pass, when the LORD shall
have done to my lord according to all the good that
he hath spoken concerning thee, and shall have
appointed thee ruler over Israel;
That this shall be no grief unto thee, nor offence of
heart unto my lord, either that thou hast shed blood
causeless, or that my lord hath avenged himself: but
when the LORD shall have dealt well with my lord,
then remember thine handmaid.
1 Samuel 25:26-31

Abigail was a woman prepared, physically, emotionally and spiritually for a very real threat against her home. She was wise in that as David and Saul were warring, she believed what God's prophet Samuel had said. David was God's appointed king.

Abigail had a bounty of provisions ready for feasting during the season of sheep shearing and harvesting, as was the custom. But the bounty she took David in no way cleaned out her stores for when she returned home, she found Nabal feasting like a king and intoxicated.

And Abigail came to Nabal; and, behold, he held a
feast in his house, like the feast of a king; and
Nabal's heart was merry within him, for he was
very drunken: wherefore she told him nothing, less
or more, until the morning light.
1 Samuel 25:36

Like wisdom's woman, discerning Abigail provided nourishment for the body and soul of her household.

MODERN WORLD

Current wars and armed conflicts as of July 2014:

Syria, Afghanistan, Iraq

Pakistan, Nigeria, D.R. Congo

South Sudan, Israel/Gaza, Ukraine

Central African Republic (CAR), India

Mali, The Philippines, Russia

Somalia, Sudan, Yemen[2]

As Israel and Jerusalem are chosen by the Lord throughout the Bible, let us consider the climate of the Holy Land.

> *And when ye shall see Jerusalem compassed with*
> *armies, then know that the desolation thereof is*
> *nigh...*
> *For these be the days of vengeance, that all things*
> *which are written may be fulfilled.*
> *Luke 21:20, 22*

The current war is raging in Gaza, and as has become the usual, Israel is again bearing the condemnation.

War-weary Christians might remain silent on war but the Bible is clear how much God loves the Jewish people and has a divine plan and purpose for Israel. The Lord calls us to love Israel and the Jewish people as He loves them.

> *And I will bless them that bless thee, and curse him*
> *that curseth thee: and in thee shall all families of the*
> *earth be blessed.*
> *Genesis 12:3*

Israel and Israeli's of all ethnicities need our prayers and support, let's seek God's blessing and bless them.

TAKING IT TO HEART

Just as the Lord had a word for David, He has always had a word and love for Israel. He also has a word for each of us individually. Like Abigail we can heed His word, and have our hearts and homes ready in the face of war.

The wars are progressing. The escalation touches our lives at a daily rate leaving us with an almost numbness. We are inundated with violence.

So many young men and women depart. Some return suffering physically, emotionally, and spiritually. We need to be aware of post-traumatic stress and the epidemic of depression that follows the young home.

As these wars increase are we numbing ourselves, or are we aware that these young men and women may need nourishment of the soul, as do their families?

The Lord tells us not to be troubled, that these wars are inevitable. He wants us to trust in Him. He is not saying we should harden our hearts.

Just as David and his men needed respect and nourishment of the body and soul, so do our own.

We can be ready for the seasons of war, to the best of our abilities. We can pray for those we know who serve, or have served in the military, and for their family members.

Missionaries and their families are also facing very serious threat and need. Support for missionaries has dwindled over recent years. These spiritual warriors need our prayers, as do their families.

PERSONAL APPLICATION

As the battles rage around us, we can consider what is happening in our world right now, consider what is prophesied and how best to invest in our future in wisdom.

FAITH

What can we do to build/protect our faith?

Believe God's word: Jesus is coming.

Daily prayer and praise.

Pray for yourself. When we are filled with the Lord's love and grace, and cleansed from our daily sins our prayers for others are clearer, bolder. To give others our best we must seek the throne of grace for ourselves.

Let our hearts not grow numb with the daily acts of war. Let us pray to be sensitive to the very real pain of God's people and to have strength, discernment and wisdom in the face of war.

Read scripture and believe His promises. Jesus told us not to be afraid.

> *Let not your heart be troubled: ye believe in*
> *God, believe also in me.*
> *John 14:1*

Consider how to be a good steward of your household in regard to your faith.

LOVE

What can we do to build/protect our love?

Speak blessings and prayers over your family and home.

Blessings over family members, and those we know who serve the Lord. Like David being chased by Saul, those we love often face persecution and attack from the evil one. Let's cover them in prayer.

You know your family like no other, their strengths, weaknesses, pain and promise. The prayers and blessing you speak over them may be the only ones they receive this day.

Include those you know in the military, Pastors and those who serve Christ during this time of violence and turmoil in the world. Pray for Pastors, Missionaries, Church members and their families.

Consider how to be a good steward of your household in regard to your love.

HOME

What can we do to build/protect our homes?

Desiring the confidence of being able to provide nourishment for our families and having a month or two of staples in our pantry is wise advise from wisdom's woman for our day. As we go on in the study let's consider the basics.

Food storage basics: **Proteins** (See Appendix II)

Consider how to be a good steward of your household in regard to the needs in your home

NOTES:

Our homes

NIV

THREE

FIELDS & FAMINE

*F*or nation shall rise against nation,
and kingdom against kingdom:
and there shall be famines,
and pestilences,
and earthquakes, in divers places.
Matthew 24:7

*S*he considereth a field,
and buyeth it:
with the fruit of her hands she planteth a
vineyard.
Proverbs 31:17

THE WARNING

The Lord's next warning is on political turmoil, famines, outbreaks and earthquakes.

Political turmoil, brings economic uncertainty, drives up prices, and induces famines from lack of planting, which in turn is followed by pestilence.

THE WOMAN

The wise woman, out of love of home and family, is investing in her future. Wisdom's woman considers the field, the right field, which will bring substance.

Is it worth her time, effort, and energy? Will the project benefit her family, her pantry, fit into the course of her life, or will it prove to be a waste of time, a vain pursuit? Will it benefit and bring fruit?

THE WISDOM

Heading warning, having foresight.

Knowing there will be political turmoil, famines, pestilence and other natural disasters such as earthquakes, wisdom heeds forewarning and seeks to bring fruit into her home.

THE WORD

How can one bear fruit in fields of famine? It all begins with faith, abiding in Christ. Consider the vine.

> *Abide in me, and I in you. As the branch cannot*
> *bear fruit of itself, except it abide in the vine; no*
> *more can ye, except ye abide in me.*
> *I am the vine, ye are the branches: He that abideth*
> *in me, and I in him, the same bringeth forth much*
> *fruit: for without me ye can do nothing.*
> *John 15:4-5*

Heading the warning of famine is clearly addressed in the Bible. Joseph, forewarned of the drought, set aside provisions during seven years for the prophesied coming famine.

> *And in the seven plenteous years the earth brought*
> *forth by handfuls.*
> *And he gathered up all the food of the seven years,*
> *which were in the land of Egypt, and laid up the*
> *food in the cities: the food of the field, which was*
> *round about every city, laid he up in the same.*
> *And Joseph gathered corn as the sand of the sea, very*
> *much, until he left numbering; for it was without*
> *number.*
> *Genesis 41:47-49*

His wisdom and obedience to the Lord's revelation was life and kindness to those in very real need.

BIBLICAL WOMAN

Bible study: Naomi

Reading: The Book of Ruth

To consider:

Naomi's husband Elimelech took his family from Bethlehem (which means house of bread), to the country of Moab (which means ease) because famine had come to the land. They lived there for ten years. During this time, first Naomi's husband died then both of her sons.

The physical famine of Bethlehem was nothing to the devastating personal famine she would suffer in Moab. She was in a land of idolaters and the men in her life, her heart's joy, her husband, then her sons, were gone one after another.

The Lord then called His beloved Naomi home. How? With word of fertile fields, bread.

> *Then she arose with her daughters in law, that she*
> *might return from the country of Moab: for she had*
> *heard in the country of Moab how that the LORD*
> *had visited his people in giving them bread.*
> *Ruth 1:6*

Her story is one of turmoil in Nations, famine and earthquakes and pestilence of the heart and soul.

But a wounded soul can still bear fruit.

In the midst of grief, Naomi may have called herself bitter, but her heart was such that Ruth cleaved to her, her people, and the Lord God. That Naomi showed God's love, and kept her faith in the Lord while in Moab is evident:

> *And Ruth said, Intreat me not to leave thee, or to*
> *return from following after thee: for whither thou*
> *goest, I will go; and where thou lodgest, I will lodge:*
> *thy people shall be my people, and thy God my God:*
> *Where thou diest, will I die, and there will I be*
> *buried: the LORD do so to me, and more also, if*
> *ought but death part thee and me.*
> *Ruth 1:16, 17*

Naomi was a fruitful vine, bringing God fruit when all was terribly lost. No matter the spiritual, emotional and physical famine that scourged away at the very heart of her life, she knew the Lord.

*And she said unto them, Call me not Naomi, call
me Mara: for the Almighty hath dealt very bitterly
with me.
I went out full, and the LORD hath brought me
home again empty: why then call ye me Naomi,
seeing the LORD hath testified against me, and the
Almighty hath afflicted me?*
Ruth 1:20, 21

In her despair, she gave Him credit and blame for all things.

As did wisdom's woman, precious Naomi, even scarred by famine, brought fruit because her eyes were on the Lord.

When all seems lost, the relationship we have with the Lord will shine through the pain. When we are despondent as Naomi, and unable to see through the darkness, we must wait. He will give us hope, and restore us.

He will bring fruit in the midst of famine.

They that sow in tears shall reap in joy.
Psalms 126:5

MODERN WORLD

Famines following political conflict, bringing pestilence in 2014.

South Sudan: "Famine and genocide threaten to engulf nation as ethnic violence puts millions of people at risk of starvation and disease."[3]

Somalia[4]

Central African Republic (CAR)[5]

The Ebola outbreak in West Africa.[6]

"Pakistan, war, polio, earthquakes, flooding and famine."[7]

Political conflict touches the lives of the people of the country. America is not exempt. Our political ugliness has left a contemptuous uncertain shadow over the Nation.

There are people who are in politics for the right reasons. They need our prayers and support.

TAKING IT TO HEART

Wisdom's call is to consider the fields in our life, and to see the fruit. We can:

- Head the warning as Joseph did.

- Have faith that the Lord will bring fruit.

Like Naomi, we can get caught up in the turmoil of life, but we must never stop looking to the Lord.

If we are blaming Him, or praising Him through the pain, just keep looking at Him. He knows you. He will see you through.

PERSONAL APPLICATION

As the world brings suffering around us, we can heed forewarning and prepare. We can consider the fields of our life: Spiritually-faith, emotionally-love, and physically-home.

FAITH

What can we do to build/protect our faith?

> *But that on the good ground are they, which in an*
> *honest and good heart, having heard the word, keep*
> *it, and bring forth fruit with patience.*
> *Luke 8:15*

Like Naomi we can keep our eyes on the Lord, through all the seasons of our life. If we keep our eyes on Him, He will bring fruit in seasons of famine.

Prayer:

> *Give us this day our daily bread.*
> *Matthew 6:11*

Promise:

> *He shall dwell on high: his place of defence shall be*
> *the munitions of rocks: bread shall be given him; his*
> *waters shall be sure.*
> *Isaiah 33:16*

List ways to assess the impending spiritual needs, being forewarned of suffering and what it can do to faith.

LOVE

What can we do to build/protect our love?

Suffering can bring bitterness of heart, which if left unchecked can grow into hardheartedness.

List ways to assess the impending emotional needs of others, being forewarned of suffering and what it can do to love.

HOME

What can we do to build/protect our homes?

In seasons of hunger the provisions we set aside will be available for hospitality to others as well as ourselves. Only the Lord knows whom He may send to your door, children, the elderly, let's prepare thoughtfully.

Food storage basics: **Grains** (See Appendix II)

List ways to assess the impending physical needs, being forewarned of suffering and what it can do to our homes.

NOTES:

NOTES:

FOUR

STRENGTH & SORROW

*A*ll these are the beginning of sorrows.
Matthew 24:7-8

*S*he girdeth her loins with strength,
and strengtheneth her arms.
Proverbs 31:17

THE WARNING

The Lord's next statement is on the beginning of sorrows. It is also called the beginning of the birth pangs.

The culmination of events combined across the world, intensifying in degree has an outcome, a birth, a result. In the season of sorrow we can remember this, the Lord will bring about His purpose.

THE WOMAN

The woman of wisdom girds herself. She is a protective keeper of her home and family.

She strengthens herself for the future.

THE WISDOM

The intensifying sorrow of the birth pains should both urge and persuade us to be hedging our families and to be steadfast keepers of the home.

THE WORD

With the aforementioned pain is the prophesied trouble and temptation of idolatrous behavior.

> *This know also, that in the last days perilous times shall come.*
> *For men shall be <u>lovers of their own selves</u>, covetous, boasters, proud, blasphemers, disobedient to parents, unthankful, unholy,*
> *Without natural affection, trucebreakers, false accusers, incontinent, fierce, despisers of those that are good,*
> *Traitors, heady, highminded, lovers of pleasures more than lovers of God;*
> *Having a form of godliness, but denying the power thereof: from such turn away.*
> *For of this sort are they which creep into houses, and lead captive silly women laden with sins, led away with divers lusts,*
> *Ever learning, and never able to come to the knowledge of the truth.*
> *2 Timothy 3:1-7*

As we consider the deception, wars, famines pestilence and natural disasters that are coming upon the word, we must also consider and acknowledge the attack on the soul.

BIBLICAL WOMAN

Bible study: Ruth

Reading: The Book of Ruth

To consider:

Ruth, a woman afflicted by the sorrow of losing her husband, found strength when faced with the reality of losing Naomi and being left in a life of idolatry in Moab.

She humbly and purposefully, chose the God of Israel and was redeemed. She clung to fragile Naomi and crossed the wilderness to meet her Kinsman Redeemer, Boaz.

> *Then she fell on her face, and bowed herself to the*
> *ground, and said unto him, Why have I found grace*
> *in thine eyes, that thou shouldest take knowledge of*
> *me, seeing I am a stranger?*
> *And Boaz answered and said unto her, It hath fully*
> *been shewed me, all that thou hast done unto thy*
> *mother in law since the death of thine husband: and*
> *how thou hast left thy father and thy mother, and*
> *the land of thy nativity, and art come unto a people*
> *which thou knewest not heretofore.*
> *The LORD recompense thy work, and a full reward*
> *be given thee of the LORD God of Israel, under*
> *whose wings thou art come to trust.*
> *Ruth 2:10-12*

Ruth pressed forward in desire of the Lord and for love of Naomi. The Lord showed Ruth that her hope in Him was not in vain.

Ruth's selfless decision to follow God, and to identify herself with His people, led her to be blessed by God, and to be in the ancestry of the Savior of the world.

During her season of sorrow, Ruth maintained strength and grace, putting aside all thought for self, but thought of the one who was more vulnerable than she.

Like wisdom's woman, loyal, lovely Ruth girded herself with strength and protectively guarded the woman who shared her household.

MODERN WORLD

Being online is a near necessity in America. Job applications and posting, news, coupons, legal forms, statistics, economical entertainment etc.-online. Email? You need it.

Today's term "selfie" is a noun, a thing. Our culture embraces the selfie, it sets it up as a fun, daily part of our life. Selfies are touched up and edited and posted online daily, on all forms of social networking.

We text, tweet, tumblr, google+, linkedin, pinterest, post, promote, pine, pillage, facebook, forum, every day.

Headlines read: Facebook Read More Than the Bible[8]

Social Networking Eats Up 3+ Hours Per Day For The Average American User[9]

Socialogue: The Most Common Butterfly On Earth Is The Social Butterfly[10]

With the inclusion of the Internet into our daily lives, we are inundated with self, self-promotion and self-interest.

TAKING IT TO HEART

Social networking and self-promotion runs rampant in a world torn apart by deception, war, famine and grief.

Do we have the strength to turn aside from idolatry, like Ruth and press forward to God and hedge those who are in our household?

> *Verily, verily, I say unto you, That ye shall weep*
> *and lament, but the world shall rejoice: and ye shall*
> *be sorrowful, but your sorrow shall be turned into*
> *joy.*
> *A woman when she is in travail hath sorrow,*
> *because her hour is come: but as soon as she is*
> *delivered of the child, she remembereth no more the*
> *anguish, for joy that a man is born into the world.*
> *And ye now therefore have sorrow: but I will see*
> *you again, and your heart shall rejoice, and your joy*
> *no man taketh from you.*
> *John 16:20-22*

Let us strengthen ourselves, and each other, to cherish our family and homes, to seek the Lord and glean the fields in whatever way He calls us to.

PERSONAL APPLICATION

Knowing that the time of sorrows is approaching, how can we prepare, and hedge our families, our homes and ourselves spiritually, emotionally and physically? Let's take a moment to prayerfully apply God's word to our lives.

FAITH

What can we do to build/ protect our faith?

Pray a hedge of protection around ourselves spiritually. We can ask the Lord to keep evil far from our doorstep.

We can step away from social networking, and assess how large of a priority it is taking on our lives. Are we numbing ourselves from the pain in the world?

We can keep a close relationship with the Lord, making sure we spend more time with Him, and with those He has entrusted us, than we do on social networking.

Prayer:

> *But keep on the alert at all times, praying in order*
> *that you may have strength to escape all these things*
> *that are about to take place, and to stand before the*
> *Son of Man.*
> *Luke 21:36*

Praise:

> *The LORD is my strength and song, and he is*
> *become my salvation: he is my God, and I will*
> *prepare him an habitation; my father's God, and I*
> *will exalt him.*
> *Exodus 15:2*

Consider how to stand strong for impending spiritual needs, being forewarned of sorrow and understanding how it can affect our faith.

LOVE

What can we do to build/ protect our love?

Pray a hedge of protection around our loved ones.

Like Ruth, we can set aside our own pain, problems and pursuits and set our hearts on our Lord's promises. Standing strong for the needs of the vulnerable and our loved ones.

Consider how to stand strong for impending emotional needs, being forewarned of sorrow and understanding how it can affect those we love.

HOME

What can we do to build/protect our homes?

Pray a hedge of protection around your home.

Food storage basics: **Fruits and Vegetables** (See Appendix II)

Consider how to stand strong and prepare for impending physical needs, being forewarned of sorrow and understanding how it can affect our homes.

NOTES:

FIVE

DARKNESS & LIGHT

Then shall they deliver you up to be afflicted,
and shall kill you:
and ye shall be hated of all nations for my name's
sake.
Matthew 24:9

She perceiveth that her merchandise is good:
her candle goeth not out by night.
Proverbs 31:18

THE WARNING

The Lord warns us that we will be delivered up to affliction, some even to death and that we will be hated for His name's sake.

THE WOMAN

Wisdom's woman perceives, she senses. She is surrounded by light even in the night. Night is a term used for tribulation.

THE WISDOM

What but God's Holy word and spirit can give light in the face of evil and persecution? Let's keep our lamps filled.

THE WORD

*Then shall the kingdom of heaven be likened unto
ten virgins, which took their lamps, and went forth
to meet the bridegroom.
And five of them were wise, and five were foolish.
They that were foolish took their lamps, and took no
oil with them:
But the wise took oil in their vessels with their
lamps.
While the bridegroom tarried, they all slumbered
and slept.
And at midnight there was a cry made, Behold, the
bridegroom cometh; go ye out to meet him.
Then all those virgins arose, and trimmed their
lamps.
And the foolish said unto the wise, Give us of your
oil; for our lamps are gone out.
But the wise answered, saying, Not so; lest there be
not enough for us and you: but go ye rather to them
that sell, and buy for yourselves.
And while they went to buy, the bridegroom came;
and they that were ready went in with him to the
marriage: and the door was shut.
Afterward came also the other virgins, saying, Lord,
Lord, open to us.
But he answered and said, Verily I say unto you, I
know you not.
Watch therefore, for ye know neither the day nor the
hour wherein the Son of man cometh.
Matthew 25:1-13*

We are to remain watchful, ready, keep in the presence of the Lord, filled
with the Holy Spirit, and keeping our lamps lit.

BIBLICAL WOMAN

Bible study: Mary Magdalene

Reading: Matthew 27:56, 61, 28:1, Mark 15:40, 47; 16:1-19, Luke 8:2; 24:1-12, John 19:25; 20:1-18

To consider:

Mary Magdalene, a woman who had once been beset and tormented by seven devils (evil spirits), was delivered from the excruciating darkness of spiritual oppression. She clung to Jesus, who delivered her from the evil she suffered, and served Him without looking back.

Mary Magdalene, filled with light and by the strength of redemption, stood by the cross, near the side of the Lord's Mother Mary, enduring the earth's darkest hour as Jesus shed His blood.

> *Now when the centurion, and they that were with him, watching Jesus, saw the earthquake, and those things that were done, they feared greatly, saying, Truly this was the Son of God.*
> *And many women were there beholding afar off, which followed Jesus from Galilee, ministering unto him:*
> *Among which was Mary Magdalene, and Mary the mother of James and Joses, and the mother of Zebedee's children.*
> *Matthew 27:54-56*

Afterward, heartbroken, she was outside His tomb.

> *But Mary stood without at the sepulchre weeping: and as she wept, she stooped down, and looked into the sepulchre,*
> *And seeth two angels in white sitting, the one at the head, and the other at the feet, where the body of Jesus had lain.*
> *And they say unto her, Woman, why weepest thou? She saith unto them, Because they have taken away my Lord, and I know not where they have laid him.*
> *And when she had thus said, she turned herself back, and saw Jesus standing, and knew not that it was Jesus.*
> *Jesus saith unto her, Woman, why weepest thou? whom seekest thou? She, supposing him to be the*

> *gardener, saith unto him, Sir, if thou have borne*
> *him hence, tell me where thou hast laid him, and I*
> *will take him away.*
> *Jesus saith unto her, Mary. She turned herself, and*
> *saith unto him, Rabboni; which is to say, Master.*
> *John 20:11-16*

She knew the reality of the darkness and she knew the reality of being redeemed from it to receive the Light. Beautiful Mary chose and clung to the Light.

MODERN WORLD

2014: Affliction, murder and persecution of Christians.

ISIS (or ISIL)'s, recent ultimatum to thousands of Christians is to convert or die, pay a special tax or to leave with only the clothes on their backs. They have no mercy for anyone of the Judeo-Christian faith.

The Islamic State is attempting to literally decimate Christianity. Recently they have taken sledgehammers to the tomb of the prophet Jonah. The churches have been destroyed or occupied and their crosses removed. It is reported that approximately 1,500 Christian manuscripts have been destroyed. Thousands of fleeing people were recently trapped on Sinjar Mountain, which was said in local legend to be the final resting place of Noah's ark.

The Islamic State have made their evil intentions towards the Judeo-Christian communities very clear to all.

Recent Headlines:

"A New Caliphate?"[11]

Christian persecution rankings; Where Christian persecution exists/World Watch List[12]

"ISIS is beheading children, raping women, and killing scores of Christians in Iraq. They are also warning Christians to convert or be massacred. At the same time, ISIS jihadists are crucifying Christians and others in Syria, and the bloody civil war in Syria has left 170,000 dead and created millions of refugees fleeing for safety."[13]

Iraq and Syria have experienced devastating atrocities against Christians.14

Despite the atrocities and being hounded unto death, these precious souls cling to Christ.

They desperately need our prayers, our outcry at their treatment, and our support.

TAKING IT TO HEART

> *The light of the body is the eye: if therefore thine eye*
> *be single, thy whole body shall be full of light.*
> *But if thine eye be evil, thy whole body shall be full*
> *of darkness. If therefore the light that is in thee be*
> *darkness, how great is that darkness!   No man can*
> *serve two masters: for either he will hate the one,*
> *and love the other; or else he will hold to the one,*
> *and despise the other. Ye cannot serve God and*
> *mammon.*
> *Matthew 6.:22-24*

Wisdom's woman is filled with light, the Lord's Holy Spirit, His Holy word, and is not letting sin (darkness) enter back into her life. She is repenting, overcoming and letting her light shine.

She, like Mary, will stand strong on that day.

PERSONAL APPLICATION

Knowing that the time of darkness and persecution is upon us, how can we prepare? Let's take a moment to prayerfully apply God's word to our lives.

FAITH

What can we do to build/protect our faith?

Prayer: Pray for understanding and direction.

> *He revealeth the deep and secret things: he knoweth*
> *what is in the darkness, and the light dwelleth with*
> *him.*
> *Daniel 2:22*

Pray for the persecuted, that they may be comforted and encouraged. Pray that those bringing darkness and grief upon our brothers and sisters in Christ would be convicted and turn away from their evil deeds to find Christ, that they would understand that Jesus is the prophesied light.

> *Then spake Jesus again unto them, saying, I am the*
> *light of the world: he that followeth me shall not*
> *walk in darkness, but shall have the light of life.*
> *John 8:12*

Consider how to clearly perceive the times, and keep your light shining during the darkness of persecution, understanding how persecution can affect faith.

LOVE

What can we do to build/protect our love?

Let us cling to Holy love as did Mary Magdalene. Let's let our loved ones be confident that nothing in this world would change the love we have for them. Let's show the love of Christ.

Consider how to clearly perceive the times, and keep your light shining during the darkness of persecution, understanding how persecution can affect our love and families.

HOME

What can we do to build/protect our homes?

Be hospitable. Ready and willing to open our warm homes to receive and assist our brothers and sisters in Christ.

Food storage basics: **Quick Meals** (See Appendix II)

Also to remember:

Emergency provisions for car.

Consider how to clearly perceive the times, and keep your light shining during the darkness of persecution, understanding how persecution can affect our homes.

NOTES:

SIX

OFFENSE & COMPASSION

*A*nd then shall many be offended,
and shall betray one another,
and shall hate one another.
Matthew 24:10

*S*he layeth her hands to the spindle, and her
hands hold the distaff.
She stretcheth out her hand to the poor; yea,
she reacheth forth her hands to the needy.
Proverbs 31:19,20

THE WARNING

The Lord's next warning is of offenses, betrayal and hate.

There is a spirit of hate permeating society. Rudeness, crude humor, and mockery can be found even on the evening news. The days of polite society are slipped away into the night. Openly offending others and shamelessly gloating over betrayal is commonplace.

THE WOMAN

Wisdom's woman is focused on laying hands to her task, stretching a hand to the poor, reaching out to the needy.

With a heart full of compassion and following with action, wisdom's woman defies the evil of the day.

THE WISDOM

Hardheartedness may abound but if we see it for what it is and don't embrace it, but reject it, and choose to live in love and charity, we can minister to the real need of those suffering all around us.

THE WORD

We are called to show God's love. The Bible makes this very clear.

*For I was an hungred, and ye gave me meat: I was
thirsty, and ye gave me drink: I was a stranger, and
ye took me in:
Naked, and ye clothed me: I was sick, and ye visited
me: I was in prison, and ye came unto me.
Then shall the righteous answer him, saying, Lord,
when saw we thee an hungred, and fed thee? or
thirsty, and gave thee drink?
When saw we thee a stranger, and took thee in? or
naked, and clothed thee?
Or when saw we thee sick, or in prison, and came
unto thee?
And the King shall answer and say unto them,
Verily I say unto you, Inasmuch as ye have done it
unto one of the least of these my brethren, ye have
done it unto me.
Matthew 25:35-40*

Charity is love.

*Though I speak with the tongues of men and of
angels, and have not charity, I am become as
sounding brass, or a tinkling cymbal.
And though I have the gift of prophecy, and
understand all mysteries, and all knowledge; and
though I have all faith, so that I could remove
mountains, and have not charity, I am nothing.
And though I bestow all my goods to feed the poor,
and though I give my body to be burned, and have
not charity, it profiteth me nothing.
Charity suffereth long, and is kind; charity envieth
not; charity vaunteth not itself, is not puffed up,
Doth not behave itself unseemly, seeketh not her
own, is not easily provoked, thinketh no evil;
Rejoiceth not in iniquity, but rejoiceth in the truth;
Beareth all things, believeth all things, hopeth all
things, endureth all things.
Charity never faileth: but whether there be
prophecies, they shall fail; whether there be tongues,*

they shall cease; whether there be knowledge, it shall
vanish away.
For we know in part, and we prophesy in part.
But when that which is perfect is come, then that
which is in part shall be done away.
When I was a child, I spake as a child, I understood
as a child, I thought as a child: but when I became
a man, I put away childish things.
For now we see through a glass, darkly; but then
face to face: now I know in part; but then shall I
know even as also I am known.
And now abideth faith, hope, charity, these three;
but the greatest of these is charity.
1 Corinthians 13

And charity after all, begins at home. If there is need or want in our own families we are called to intervene.

If any man or woman that believeth have widows,
let them relieve them, and let not the church be
charged; that it may relieve them that are widows
indeed.
1 Timothy 5:16

BIBLICAL WOMAN

Bible study: Tabitha (Dorcas)

Reading: Acts 9:36-42.

To consider:

> *Now there was at Joppa a certain disciple named*
> *Tabitha, which by interpretation is called Dorcas:*
> *this woman was full of good works and almsdeeds*
> *which she did.*
> *And it came to pass in those days, that she was sick,*
> *and died: whom when they had washed, they laid*
> *her in an upper chamber.*
> *And forasmuch as Lydda was nigh to Joppa, and the*
> *disciples had heard that Peter was there, they sent*
> *unto him two men, desiring him that he would not*
> *delay to come to them.*
> *Then Peter arose and went with them. When he*
> *was come, they brought him into the upper*
> *chamber: and all the widows stood by him weeping,*
> *and shewing the coats and garments which Dorcas*
> *made, while she was with them.*
> *But Peter put them all forth, and kneeled down,*
> *and prayed; and turning him to the body said,*
> *Tabitha, arise. And she opened her eyes: and when*
> *she saw Peter, she sat up.*
> *And he gave her his hand, and lifted her up, and*
> *when he had called the saints and widows, presented*
> *her alive.*
> *And it was known throughout all Joppa; and many*
> *believed in the Lord.*
> *Acts 9:36-42*

Generous, kindly Tabitha is the only woman in scripture to be specifically called a disciple. She was a sincere disciple of Christ, obeying His commands and ministering to the needy in such a way that it grieved the Christian community to lose her, and touched the heart of Peter to bring her back.

Tabitha, like wisdom's woman, put her hand to the spindle and made clothes for the poor. Her heart belonged to Christ and her thoughts were on serving God, therefore her heart and outstretched hands were for the poor and helpless.

MODERN WORLD

The economic uncertainty in the world is creating a precarious desperation in society. People are aggressively seeking advancement and stability, even at the cost of offending others. Even some churches are becoming fiscally minded to all shame.

Let's consider the current statistics of poverty in America in the current year, 2014:

Poverty rate in America is at 15 percent.[15]

50 million Americans live below the poverty line.[16]

25% of American population are living in poverty stricken areas.[17]

9.8 million workers unemployed but there are only 4.6 million job openings.[18]

TAKING IT TO HEART

When the world is full of cutthroats, scoffers, the spirit of hate, advancement and dissatisfaction, you know someone who is hurting. You know someone who has been left by his or her spouse, or sacked from his or her job. There is pain all around us.

> *How blessed is he who considers the helpless; the*
> *Lord will deliver him in a day of trouble.*
> *The Lord will protect him, and keep him alive, and*
> *he shall be called blessed upon the earth; and do not*
> *give him over to the desire of his enemies.*
> *Psalms 41:1-2*

Like wisdom's woman, we can head and follow Christ and minister to the needs of the suffering. We can be both doers and hearers of his word.

PERSONAL APPLICATION

Knowing that the day is hostile and peoples needs are high how can we extend our hands to those suffering in economic uncertainty?

FAITH

What can we do to build/ protect our faith?

Pray for those you know are suffering, knowing that want can wear down the heart and soul.

Act in faith.

Knowing that tough times are upon us, we can make a plan, and carry out our faith in action. We can donate, help collect or distribute food. If we are very busy and have the means, we can write that check.

List ways you are inspired to live in love and charity, in regard to your faith.

LOVE

What can we do to build/ protect our love?

Act in love.

We can follow Christ and let His love shine by showing mercy and charity for others, and extend our hands and hearts to the poor.

List ways you are inspired to live in love and charity, in regard to your family.

HOME

What can we do to build/ protect our homes?

Check needs and conditions of our own family's clothing with our eye to the future.

Everyday clothing: Necessities plus.

Seasonal clothing:

Jackets, sweaters, warm socks, and boots etc. depending on climate.

While we think of the needs of our household we can readily help those who are in need. As we go through fulfilling and preparing for the needs of our family we can set aside to give to the poor.

For the pantry: **List of services** (See Appendix II)

A list of numbers/times/places of community services in your area.

List ways you are inspired to live in love and charity, in regard to your home.

NOTES:

SEVEN

THE FALSE & FORGIVEN

And many false prophets shall rise,
and shall deceive many.
Matthew 24:11

She is not afraid of the snow for her household:
for all her household are clothed with scarlet.
She maketh herself coverings of tapestry; her
clothing is silk and purple.
Proverbs 31:21-22

THE WARNING

The Lord's next warning is on false prophets, who will deceive many. They will enter our churches, teaching questionable doctrinal theories, even heresies.

THE WOMAN

Wisdom's woman is not afraid. She is covered, as is her household.

THE WISDOM

When the precious blood of Christ covers our sins, we are forgiven, redeemed and by the power of the Holy Spirit we can see though the false.

THE WORD

Beware of false prophets, which come to you in
sheep's clothing, but inwardly they are ravening
wolves.
Ye shall know them by their fruits. Do men gather
grapes of thorns, or figs of thistles?
Matthew 7:15,16

But there were false prophets also among the people,
even as there shall be false teachers among you, who
privily shall bring in damnable heresies, even
denying the Lord that bought them, and bring upon
themselves swift destruction.
And many shall follow their pernicious ways; by
reason of whom the way of truth shall be evil spoken
of.
And through covetousness shall they with feigned
words make merchandise of you: whose judgment
now of a long time lingereth not, and their
damnation slumbereth not.
For if God spared not the angels that sinned, but
cast them down to hell, and delivered them into
chains of darkness, to be reserved unto judgment;
And spared not the old world, but saved Noah the
eighth person, a preacher of righteousness, bringing
in the flood upon the world of the ungodly;...
While they promise them liberty, they themselves are
the servants of corruption: for of whom a man is
overcome, of the same is he brought in bondage.
For if after they have escaped the pollutions of the
world through the knowledge of the Lord and
Saviour Jesus Christ, they are again entangled
therein, and overcome, the latter end is worse with
them than the beginning.
For it had been better for them not to have known
the way of righteousness, than, after they have
known it, to turn from the holy commandment
delivered unto them.
2 Peter 2:1-5, 19-21

Beloved, believe not every spirit, but try the spirits

whether they are of God: because many false
prophets are gone out into the world.
Hereby know ye the Spirit of God: Every spirit that
confesseth that Jesus Christ is come in the flesh is of
God:
And every spirit that confesseth not that Jesus Christ
is come in the flesh is not of God: and this is that
spirit of antichrist, whereof ye have heard that it
should come; and even now already is it in the
world.
Ye are of God, little children, and have overcome
them: because greater is he that is in you, than he
that is in the world.
They are of the world: therefore speak they of the
world, and the world heareth them.
We are of God: he that knoweth God heareth us; he
that is not of God heareth not us. Hereby know we
the spirit of truth, and the spirit of error.
1 John 4:1-6

What is said about God and His word is of the utmost importance; by this fruit we will know them for who they are.

BIBLICAL WOMAN

Bible study: Lydia

Reading: Acts 16:6-40

To consider:

Lydia, who traded in purple dye, resisted the false religion of her city, and believed in the God of Israel.

> *And on the sabbath we went out of the city by a*
> *river side, where prayer was wont to be made; and*
> *we sat down, and spake unto the women which*
> *resorted thither.*
> *And a certain woman named Lydia, a seller of*
> *purple, of the city of Thyatira, which worshipped*
> *God, heard us: whose heart the Lord opened, that*
> *she attended unto the things which were spoken of*
> *Paul.*
> *And when she was baptized, and her household, she*
> *besought us, saying, If ye have judged me to be*
> *faithful to the Lord, come into my house, and abide*
> *there. And she constrained us.*
> *Acts 16:13-15*

Lydia was at the river seeking the Lord as there wasn't a synagogue in Philippi. That's where Paul also went to pray. She was Paul's first convert in Europe, and her baptism was a public confession.

Lydia was a businesswoman, and the mistress of her household. She was hospitable, and supportive of others. Though it was her household alone, her loving, faithful belief in God, and generous nature cannot be denied.

The Lord knows us no matter where we worship or seek Him. He will meet us. Lovely Lydia received the gospel and was baptized by water, and by the fruit of her witness and faith, her whole household was saved.

Lydia, like wisdom's woman, was clothed in purple, but the blood of Christ covered her sins and that of her household.

MODERN WORLD

Today there are many dangerous theologies that have Christians concerned.

Replacement theology. Here is what Paul has to say.

*Boast not against the branches. But if thou boast,
thou bearest not the root, but the root thee.
Thou wilt say then, The branches were broken off,
that I might be graffed in.
Well; because of unbelief they were broken off, and
thou standest by faith. Be not highminded, but fear:
For if God spared not the natural branches, take
heed lest he also spare not thee.
Behold therefore the goodness and severity of God:
on them which fell, severity; but toward thee,
goodness, if thou continue in his goodness: otherwise
thou also shalt be cut off.
And they also, if they abide not still in unbelief,
shall be graffed in: for God is able to graff them in
again.
For if thou wert cut out of the olive tree which is
wild by nature, and wert graffed contrary to nature
into a good olive tree: how much more shall these,
which be the natural branches, be graffed into their
own olive tree?
For I would not, brethren, that ye should be
ignorant of this mystery, lest ye should be wise in
your own conceits; that blindness in part is
happened to Israel, until the fulness of the Gentiles
be come in.
And so all Israel shall be saved: as it is written,
There shall come out of Sion the Deliverer, and
shall turn away ungodliness from Jacob:
For this is my covenant unto them, when I shall
take away their sins.
As concerning the gospel, they are enemies for your
sakes: but as touching the election, they are beloved
for the fathers' sakes.
For the gifts and calling of God are without
repentance.
Romans 11:18-29*

*For the LORD will not cast off his people, neither
will he forsake his inheritance.
Psalms 94:14*

God's covenant with Israel still stands. God is not a covenant breaker. To besmirch God's character is a sin, an unloving blasphemy.

Predestination theology:

> *Who will have <u>all men to be saved</u>, and to come*
> *unto the knowledge of the truth.*
> *For there is one God, and one mediator between*
> *God and men, the man Christ Jesus;*
> *<u>Who gave himself a ransom for all</u>, to be testified in*
> *due time.*
> *1 Timothy 2:4-6*

Jesus took the cross for all mankind. To say otherwise cheapens grace and is another cruel, conceited blasphemy.

TAKING IT TO HEART

Are we listening to people who are speaking as Pharisees in our day? Let's listen to the Lord's admonition:

> *And he spake this parable unto certain which*
> *trusted in themselves that they were righteous, and*
> *despised others:*
> *Two men went up into the temple to pray; the one a*
> *Pharisee, and the other a publican.*
> *The Pharisee stood and prayed thus with himself,*
> *God, I thank thee, that I am not as other men are,*
> *extortioners, unjust, adulterers, or even as this*
> *publican.*
> *I fast twice in the week, I give tithes of all that I*
> *possess.*
> *And the publican, standing afar off, would not lift*
> *up so much as his eyes unto heaven, but smote upon*
> *his breast, saying, God be merciful to me a sinner.*
> *I tell you, this man went down to his house justified*
> *rather than the other: for every one that exalteth*
> *himself shall be abased; and he that humbleth*
> *himself shall be exalted.*
> *Luke 18:9-14*

We can rejoice in our salvation, but a woman of discernment understands humility, she is a human being, a forgiven sinner, saved by grace.

PERSONAL APPLICATION

Knowing that the time is thick with deception and heresies, how should we prepare? Let's take a moment to prayerfully apply God's word to our lives.

FAITH

What can we do to build/protect our faith?

All her household is covered in scarlet: The precious blood of Christ. When we stay in the word and walk with the Lord, confessing our sins and living our lives in faith, false theologies and prophecies will not sit well with the Holy Spirit.

Some people might feel uncomfortable, an inner rejection even, as they listen to people speak. Every spiritual warning can and should be checked with scripture. If you doubt it is His voice, check.

> *But ye believe not, because ye are not of my sheep, as*
> *I said unto you.*
> *My sheep hear my voice, and I know them, and*
> *they follow me:*
> *And I give unto them eternal life; and they shall*
> *never perish, neither shall any man pluck them out*
> *of my hand.*
> *My Father, which gave them me, is greater than*
> *all; and no man is able to pluck them out of my*
> *Father's hand.*
> *I and my Father are one.*
> *John 10:26-30*

Consider how questionable doctrines affect the witness and faith of the body of Christ.

LOVE

What can we do to build/ protect our love?

Lydia provides a wonderful example of love, her home is open to believers, she shares her faith and her first thoughts after conversion were toward her household. Her household, her family, was saved.

Consider how questionable doctrines affect the love in the body of Christ.

HOME

What can we do to build/ protect our homes?

As Lydia was baptized we are going to focus on water storage. The experts say it is often little thought of, but of the highest priority for survival.

Food storage basics: **Water** (See Appendix II)

Linen closet:

Blankets, towels and other adequate coverings.

Consider how questionable doctrines affect the attitudes in our homes and families.

NOTES:

EIGHT

COLDNESS & KINDNESS

*A*nd because iniquity shall abound,
the love of many shall wax cold.
Matthew 24:12

*H*er husband is known in the gates, when he
sitteth among the elders of the land.
She maketh fine linen,
and selleth it; and delivereth girdles unto the
merchant.
Strength and honour are her clothing; and she
shall rejoice in time to come.
She openeth her mouth with wisdom; and in her
tongue is the law of kindness.
Proverbs 31:23-26

THE WARNING

The Lord's next warning is that iniquity, lawlessness, will abound and that the love of many will grow cold.

People will be hardhearted and have no respect each other, for God or His law, and sin will abound.

THE WOMAN

Wisdom's woman respects her husband, he is at the gate, and she is busy being industrious to bring support. With strength, she looks to her future and she speaks with kindness.

She loves her husband, showing him respect. She is looking to her family's future and from the outflow of her heart; she is kind with her words as well as her deeds.

THE WISDOM

In a time of disrespect, lawlessness and coldness, we can assess the day and place our trust in God, keeping our hearts and faith passionate. Which will in turn keep kindness on our lips, born of the heart.

THE WORD

Likewise, ye wives, be in subjection to your own husbands; that, if any obey not the word, they also may without the word be won by the conversation of the wives;
While they <u>behold your chaste conversation</u> coupled with fear.
Whose adorning let it not be that outward adorning of plaiting the hair, and of wearing of gold, or of putting on of apparel;
<u>But let it be the hidden man of the heart,</u> in that which is not corruptible, even the ornament of a meek and quiet spirit, which is in the sight of God of great price.
For after this manner in the old time the holy women also, who trusted in God, adorned themselves, being in subjection unto their own husbands:
Even as Sara obeyed Abraham, calling him lord: whose daughters ye are, as long as ye do well, and <u>are not afraid with any amazement.</u>
1 Peter 3:1-6

Sarah was not afraid because she trusted the Lord with her husband. When we place our trust in God with the people in our lives, we receive strength for the day.

When we prayerfully voice our concerns and fears to the Lord and then place our trust in Him, something beautiful happens, something holy; love grows.

BIBLICAL WOMAN

Bible study: Esther

Reading: The Book of Esther

To consider:

Esther's husband Ahasuerus was very well known, but she was a woman who was often alone. Let's see how the Lord helped her look to the future.

When she was alone as an orphan the Lord gave her Mordici. When she was alone in the harem the Lord gave her Hegai. When she was alone with the king the Lord gave her a husband. When she was alone in her marriage, and the death of her people was plotted, the Lord gave her a miracle.

As she entered the king's throne room alone, without a summons, facing death. God was with her.

Throughout her story, the Lord was always there. He was there in her pain. He was there in her fear. He was there in her moment of need.

Esther clung to the Lord. She had faith in Him over the happenings in her life. With her husband, her people, her life.

Whatever you face, whatever your day of trouble holds, He is there.

Esther gained the favor of Hegai, the keeper of the house of the women. As keeper of our own homes let's take a moment and see what Hegai provided her.

And the maiden pleased him, and she obtained
kindness of him; and he speedily gave her her things
for purification, with such things as belonged to her,
and seven maidens, which were meet to be given
her, out of the king's house: and he preferred her
and her maids unto the best place of the house of the
women.
Esther 2:9

He provided her with cleanliness and care. Seven maids from the palace gave her knowledge of the king's house, discernment for the days ahead. He gave her such things as belonged to her, good food. He made sure she had a good diet.

Most importantly, he gave her a separate place, a sanctuary. She did not assimilate into the life of the harem, which helped her maintain her identity and gave her a quiet place with the Lord.

Receiving the favor of Hegai, was a blessing as he ministered to her needs in a very stressful situation, and she in return respected his opinion.

> *Now when the turn of Esther, the daughter of*
> *Abihail the uncle of Mordecai, who had taken her*
> *for his daughter, was come to go in unto the king,*
> *she required nothing but what Hegai the king's*
> *chamberlain, the keeper of the women, appointed.*
> *And Esther obtained favour in the sight of all them*
> *that looked upon her.*
> *Esther 2:15*

She then received the favor of the king.

> *So Esther was taken unto king Ahasuerus into his*
> *house royal in the tenth month, which is the month*
> *Tebeth, in the seventh year of his reign.*
> *And the king loved Esther above all the women,*
> *and she obtained grace and favour in his sight more*
> *than all the virgins; so that he set the royal crown*
> *upon her head, and made her queen instead of*
> *Vashti.*
> *Esther 2:16.17*

Esther was uniquely beautiful but she had more than physical beauty, she perceived the situations in her life and put her faith in the Lord.

She displayed discernment, kindness and grace.

How she received the kindness of Hegai and the love of her husband is revealed by her character and actions even further when Haman set a plot to destroy the Jewish people.

Though she had been quiet about her faith, she feared and worshiped God.

When she was asked to question the new law put down against her people and go unbidden to the kings presence, placing her in a life or death situation, she displayed humility, love of others and courage.

> *Go, gather together all the Jews that are present in*
> *Shushan, and fast ye for me, and neither eat nor*
> *drink three days, night or day: I also and my*
> *maidens will fast likewise; and so will I go in unto*
> *the king, which is not according to the law: and if I*
> *perish, I perish.*
> *Esther 4:16*

Esther went first to the Lord. She fasted and prayed for three days, representing sincere repentance and seeking the Lord. She knew the only power to turn to was the Lord. She acted in that faith.

But the salvation of the righteous is of the LORD:
he is their strength in the time of trouble.
Psalm 37:39

When she did speak her words were thoughtful, kind, respectful but also sincere. She did not vainly flatter the king. She was direct but discreet.

In Esther's day of trouble and cold-heartedness, she displayed an absolute trust in God, acted with discretion, and spoke with wisdom and the law of kindness.

Esther, like wisdom's woman, respected her husband, spoke with the law of kindness, and by faith in God looked with strength to her future.

In our day such as this, let us place our faith in God's presence and power, look with discernment and knowledge over the happenings in our lives, and live with discretion, wisdom and kindness.

MODERN WORLD

In our day, similar to the story of Esther, is Hamas calling for an end to Israel.

Hamas, according to the Gesenius Hebrew lexicon, means violence, lawlessness, and false witness. It is uncannily comparable to the name Haman.

Haman has different meanings, however according to Hitchcock's Dictionary of Bible Names it means noise and tumult.

Hamas is a militant Islamic fundamentalist political movement that opposes peace with Israel and uses terrorism as a weapon. It seeks to create an Islamic state in place of Israel, oppresses the Palestinian people, and pioneered suicide bombing.

Like Haman's decree, Hamas' charter calls for the destruction of Israel and does not recognize Israel's legitimacy.

Throughout the world anti-Semitism is escalating.

Recent Headline August 2014

"Anti-Semitism on rise across Europe 'in worst times since the Nazis'

Experts say attacks go beyond Israel-Palestinian conflict as hate crimes strike fear into Jewish communities."[19]

Israel has the responsibility and the right to defend its citizens, of all ethnicities. As does America, and every other nation in the world.

As Christians, we should be speaking out for, and standing firmly with Israel.

TAKING IT TO HEART

When people have no tolerance for God's law (lawlessness), morality gets redefined. Iniquity becomes commonplace. Words precede deeds. Words are powerful, God spoke and there was light.

The heart of man makes itself known through the mouth.

> *Death and life are in the power of the tongue.*
> *Proverbs 15:2*

Jesus said:

> *It is not*
> *what goes into the mouth that defiles a man; but*
> *what comes out of the*
> *mouth, this defiles a man.*
> *Matthew 15:11*

In addition, we read in the Bible, with our mouths we bless and forgive:

> *And Peter calling to remembrance saith unto him,*
> *Master, behold, the fig tree which thou cursedst is*
> *withered away.*
> *And Jesus answering saith unto them, Have faith*
> *in God.*
> *For verily I say unto you, That whosoever shall say*
> *unto this mountain, Be thou removed, and be thou*
> *cast into the sea; and shall not doubt in his heart,*
> *but shall believe that those things which he saith*
> *shall come to pass; he shall have whatsoever he saith.*
> *Therefore I say unto you, What things soever ye*
> *desire, when ye pray, believe that ye receive them,*
> *and ye shall have them.*
> *And when ye stand praying, forgive, if ye have ought*
> *against any: that your Father also which is in*
> *heaven may forgive you your trespasses.*
> *But if ye do not forgive, neither will your Father*
> *which is in heaven forgive your trespasses.*
> *Mark 11:21-26*

In a time of disrespect, lawlessness and coldness, we can assess the day and place our trust in God, and keep our hearts and faith passionate, thereby maintaining grace to keep the law of kindness on our tongues.

PERSONAL APPLICATION

Knowing that the time is thick with iniquity, lawlessness, and that the love of many will grow cold, how should we prepare? Let's take a moment to prayerfully apply God's word to our lives.

FAITH

What can we do to build/protect our faith?

We can remember God's commandments, post them in our homes, and teach them to our children.

> *Thou shalt have no other gods before me.*
> *Thou shalt not make unto thee any graven image,*
> *Thou shalt not take the name of the LORD thy God*
> *in vain*
> *Remember the sabbath day, to keep it holy.*
> *Honour thy father and thy mother:*
> *Thou shalt not kill.*
> *Thou shalt not commit adultery.*
> *Thou shalt not steal.*
> *Thou shalt not bear false witness against thy*
> *neighbour.*
> *Thou shalt not covet*
> *Exodus 20:3-4,7-8,12-17*

List ways you are inspired to live in love, with words as well as in deeds, in regard to your faith.

LOVE

What can we do to build/ protect our love?

We can trust the Lord with our family members. We can trust Him in every area of their lives and not give way to fear.

We can, like Esther, trust Him with our own lives and futures.

We can practice discernment and speak kindly to those we love.

List ways you are inspired to live in love, with words as well as in deeds, in regard to your family.

HOME

What can we do to build/ protect our homes?

We can keep our homes sanctuaries of kindness. A refuge from the world, filled with love, appreciation and acceptance.

Food storage basics: **Specialty and necessities** (See Appendix II)

List ways you are inspired to live in love, with words as well as in deeds, in regard to your home.

NOTES:

NOTES:

NINE

VICTORY & VIGILANCE

*B*ut he that shall endure unto the end, the same
shall be saved.
Matthew 24:13

*S*he looketh well to the ways of her household,
and eateth not the bread of idleness.
Proverbs 31:27

THE WARNING

The Lord's next warning is of endurance to the end.

Endurance is believing and pressing on when all seems lost. It is spiritual.

THE WOMAN

Wisdom's woman is keeping an eye over the state of her household, assessing her family's needs, physically, emotionally, and spiritually. She nurtures them, and doesn't neglect them.

THE WISDOM

Endurance is fortitude, strength and resolution. We can trust in God and decide to stay the course and act in faith. He will see us through, in our faith and as nurturers and keepers of the home.

THE WORD

Jesus directs us to endure in prayer and faith.

> *And he spake a parable unto them to this end, that*
> *men ought always to pray, and not to faint;*
> *Saying, There was in a city a judge, which feared*
> *not God, neither regarded man:*
> *And there was a widow in that city; and she came*
> *unto him, saying, Avenge me of mine adversary.*
> *And he would not for a while: but afterward he*
> *said within himself, Though I fear not God, nor*
> *regard man;*
> *Yet because this widow troubleth me, I will avenge*
> *her, lest by her continual coming she weary me.*
> *And the Lord said, Hear what the unjust judge*
> *saith.*
> *And shall not God avenge his own elect, which cry*
> *day and night unto him, though he bear long with*
> *them?*
> *I tell you that he will avenge them speedily.*
> *Nevertheless when the Son of man cometh, shall he*
> *find faith on the earth?*
> *Luke 18:1-8*

The word tells us to persevere, flee from sin and pursue love and faith.

> *But thou, O man of God, flee these things; and*
> *follow after righteousness, godliness, faith, love,*
> *patience, meekness.*
> *Fight the good fight of faith, lay hold on eternal*
> *life, whereunto thou art also called, and hast*
> *professed a good profession before many witnesses.*
> *1 Timothy 6:11-12*

By obeying the word we fight the good fight of faith.

> *Now all these things happened unto them for*
> *ensamples: and they are written for our admonition,*
> *upon whom the ends of the world are come.*
> *Wherefore let him that thinketh he standeth take*
> *heed lest he fall.*
> *There hath no temptation taken you but such as is*

common to man: but God is faithful, who will not
suffer you to be tempted above that ye are able; but
will with the temptation also make a way to escape,
that ye may be able to bear it.
Wherefore, my dearly beloved, flee from idolatry.
I speak as to wise men; judge ye what I say.
1 Corinthians 10:11-15

It is wisdom to study the Bible, to read and contemplate the stories of biblical people and the word. It spiritually strengthens us, gives us understanding to endure, and reminds us of the faithfulness of God.

The horse is prepared against the day of battle: but
safety is of the LORD.
Proverbs 21:31

BIBLICAL WOMAN

Bible study: Rahab

Reading: Joshua 2:1-21, 6:17-25, Matthew 1:5, Hebrews 11:31, James 2:25

To consider:

Rahab is singled out for her active faith in the books of Hebrews and James.

> *By faith the harlot Rahab perished not with them*
> *that believed not, when she had received the spies*
> *with peace.*
> *Hebrews 11:31*

> *Ye see then how that by works a man is justified,*
> *and not by faith only.*
> *Likewise also was not Rahab the harlot justified by*
> *works, when she had received the messengers, and*
> *had sent them out another way?*
> *For as the body without the spirit is dead, so faith*
> *without works is dead also.*
> *James 2:24-26*

She is a woman who had an enduring faith and belief in God. Her life in Jericho meant nothing to her, only her family. She knew the spies that came to her door knew and followed God.

> *And she said unto the men, I know that the LORD*
> *hath given you the land, and that your terror is*
> *fallen upon us, and that all the inhabitants of the*
> *land faint because of you.*
> *For we have heard how the LORD dried up the*
> *water of the Red sea for you, when ye came out of*
> *Egypt; and what ye did unto the two kings of the*
> *Amorites, that were on the other side Jordan, Sihon*
> *and Og, whom ye utterly destroyed.*
> *And as soon as we had heard these things, our*
> *hearts did melt, neither did there remain any more*
> *courage in any man, because of you: for the LORD*
> *your God, he is God in heaven above, and in earth*
> *beneath.*
> *Joshua 2:9-11*

Rahab knew the Lord was going to bring judgment on the land. A wise woman who lives in a sinful time and place knows, and Rahab sought deliverance. The Lord sent the spies to her, out of all of the souls in Jericho. He knew her heart.

> *Now therefore, I pray you, swear unto me by the*
> *LORD, since I have shewed you kindness, that ye*
> *will also shew kindness unto my father's house, and*
> *give me a true token:*
> *And that ye will save alive my father, and my*
> *mother, and my brethren, and my sisters, and all*
> *that they have, and deliver our lives from death.*
> *And the men answered her, Our life for yours, if ye*
> *utter not this our business. And it shall be, when the*
> *LORD hath given us the land, that we will deal*
> *kindly and truly with thee.*
> *Then she let them down by a cord through the*
> *window: for her house was upon the town wall, and*
> *she dwelt upon the wall.*
> *Joshua 2:12-15*

Rahab put her hope and trust in the Lord and believed in His power and majesty. She acted in faith that the Lord would work a miracle for her and her household.

She trusted in the Lord and did as was asked in faith, tying the red cord, and was spared, as was her household.

Rahab believed that He was Almighty God and He blessed her. When the mighty walls of Jericho fell flat, her household in the wall escaped tragedy.

> *But Joshua had said unto the two men that had*
> *spied out the country, Go into the harlot's house,*
> *and bring out thence the woman, and all that she*
> *hath, as ye sware unto her.*
> *And the young men that were spies went in, and*
> *brought out Rahab, and her father, and her mother,*
> *and her brethren, and all that she had; and they*
> *brought out all her kindred, and left them without*
> *the camp of Israel.*
> *Joshua 6:22,23*

She believed and wondered at His miraculous almighty power. She testified of it. God is so good. He showed her He heard. And then He blessed her all the more.

Rahab became the wife of Salmon, and was the mother of Boaz, who married Ruth. Ruth's son was Obed, who fathered Jesse. Jesse was the father of David, through whose line Jesus was born.

Faithful Rahab, like wisdom's woman, discerned the times and looked well to her household. While the walls were falling all around her, she acted in faith and endured though it all by placing her trust in the Lord until He delivered her.

MODERN WORLD

Spiritual apathy, apostasy in the church.

*Let no man deceive you by any means: for that day
shall not come, except there come a falling away
first, and that man of sin be revealed, the son of
perdition;
2 Thessalonians 2:3*

*Now the Spirit speaketh expressly, that in the latter
times some shall depart from the faith, giving heed
to seducing spirits, and doctrines of devils;
Speaking lies in hypocrisy; having their conscience
seared with a hot iron;
1 Timothy 4:1,2*

As the seasons of sorrows are upon us some people may give up their Christian commitment. An apostasy is a general falling away from the purity of the faith. It is defined as the gradual declension, corruption, and departure from the ancient faith.

June 2014:

The Presbyterian Church USA (PCUSA) has publicly and officially turned it's back on Israel. Their General Assembly voted to divest from companies that operate in Israel.

Since this act many faith filled, Bible believing Christians and congregations have left this organization or have cut ties with it.

The Presbyterian Church USA (PCUSA) organization expresses the blatant face of apostasy in the church in our day.

According to their recently released religious demographic profile report, many of their pastors and members deny the divinity of Jesus Christ and reject numerous teachings of the Bible.[20]

TAKING IT TO HEART

Christians can discern apathy, reject it, and press forward in an enduring faith.

> *Therefore, brethren, stand fast, and hold the*
> *traditions which ye have been taught, whether by*
> *word, or our epistle.*
> *Now our Lord Jesus Christ himself, and God, even*
> *our Father, which hath loved us, and hath given us*
> *everlasting consolation and good hope through grace,*
> *Comfort your hearts, and stablish you in every good*
> *word and work.*
> *2 Thessalonians 2:14-15;*

We are able to persevere because of the power of God, the Holy Spirit, is working within us.

> *Being confident of this very thing, that he which*
> *hath begun a good work in you will perform it until*
> *the day of Jesus Christ:*
> *Philippians 1:6*

> *Now unto him that is able to keep you from falling,*
> *and to present you faultless before the presence of his*
> *glory with exceeding joy,*
> *Jude 1:24*

> *Because thou hast kept the word of my patience, I*
> *also will keep thee from the hour of temptation,*
> *which shall come upon all the world, to try them*
> *that dwell upon the earth.*
> *Behold, I come quickly: hold that fast which thou*
> *hast, that no man take thy crown.*
> *Revelations 3:10,11*

To endure to the end we must be on our guard and persistent in prayer.

> *And take heed to yourselves, lest at any time your*
> *hearts be overcharged with surfeiting, and*
> *drunkenness, and cares of this life, and so that day*
> *come upon you unawares.*
> *For as a snare shall it come on all them that dwell*

on the face of the whole earth.
Watch ye therefore, and pray always, that ye may be
accounted worthy to escape all these things that shall
come to pass, and to stand before the Son of man.
Luke 21:34-36

PERSONAL APPLICATION

Knowing that the time is thick with apathy and that a wise woman endures, how should we prepare? Let's take a moment to prayerfully apply God's word to our lives.

FAITH

What can we do to build/protect our faith?

As the times grow tougher we can press forward in faith. The world may be falling all around us, but His words should encourage us.

> *And when these things begin to come to pass, then look up, and lift up your heads; for your redemption draweth nigh.*
> *Luke 21:28*

Consider how you can avoid apathy by keeping a nurturing eye over the state of your household, and assessing the spiritual needs.

LOVE

What can we do to build/ protect our love?

Praying for our family's protection. Remembering their need for safety: physically, spiritually, and emotionally. Putting our hearts, bodies and minds to their different spiritual, physical and emotional needs. Enduring in faith for their deliverance.

Consider how you can avoid apathy by keeping a nurturing eye over the state of your household, and assessing the emotional needs.

HOME

What can we do to build/ protect our homes?

We can love our homes; pray the Lord's blessing over each room, brick and board.

Food storage basics: **Other emergency necessities** (See Appendix II)

Search out disaster preparedness websites and information. Basic preparedness website links are included in Appendix One.

Consider how you can avoid apathy by keeping a nurturing eye over the state of your household, and assessing the physical needs.

NOTES:

TEN

FINISHING & FAITH

*A*nd this gospel of the kingdom shall be preached
in all the world for a witness unto all nations; and
then shall the end come.
Matthew 24:14

*H*er children arise up, and call her blessed; her
husband also, and he praiseth her. Many
daughters have done virtuously, but thou
excellest them all. Favour is deceitful, and beauty
is vain: but a woman that feareth the LORD, she
shall be praised. Give her of the fruit of her
hands; and let her own works praise her in the
gates.
Proverbs 31:28-31

THE WARNING

The Lord's warning is that the gospel shall be preached through all the world, then the end shall come.

THE WOMAN

Wisdom's woman looks to God. As she lives her life, loves her family, provides for her home, she is inspired by, believing, and loving the Lord. She fears the Lord and it will help her and benefit her to the end.

THE WISDOM

Knowing the gospel to be preached throughout the world signifies the beginning of the end; a wise woman believes, trusts and walks in the fear of the Lord to the end.

THE WORD

I have fought a good fight, I have finished my course, I have kept the faith: Henceforth there is laid up for me a crown of righteousness, which the Lord, the righteous judge, shall give me at that day: and not to me only, but unto all them also that love his appearing.
2 Timothy 4:7-8

By faith Noah, being warned of God of things not seen as yet, moved with fear, prepared an ark to the saving of his house; by the which he condemned the world, and became heir of the righteousness which is by faith.
Hebrews 11:7

But let us, who are of the day, be sober, putting on the breastplate of faith and love; and for an helmet, the hope of salvation.
For God hath not appointed us to wrath, but to obtain salvation by our Lord Jesus Christ,
Who died for us, that, whether we wake or sleep, we should live together with him.
1 Thessalonians 5:8-10

BIBLICAL WOMAN

Sarah (Sarai)

Reading: Genesis 12:1-20, 16:1-8, 17:1-22, 18:1-15, 21:1-13, 23:1-19, 24:36,37, 25:10,12, 49:31, Isaiah 51:2, Romans 4:19, 9:9, Galatians 4:22-31, Hebrews 11:11, I Peter 3:6.

To consider:

Though we sometimes doubt our purpose in life and our value, to the Lord we are significant and he will bring us joy and laughter.

Sarai's barrenness is included in her introduction in the Bible.

> *And Abram and Nahor took them wives: the name*
> *of Abram's wife was Sarai; and the name of Nahor's*
> *wife, Milcah, the daughter of Haran, the father of*
> *Milcah, and the father of Iscah.*
> *But Sarai was barren; she had no child.*
> *Genesis 11:29-30*

Sarai had lived a full life with Abram and had not been able to conceive a child. Years passed by, and she clung to him and the Lord.

At that time, if a woman did not produce a male heir within two years it was custom, and written into many marriage contracts, that a handmaiden of the wife's choosing be provided as a surrogate mother to produce an heir.[21]

After forty plus years of marriage, and proving unable to bear a child, Sarai made the heartrending choice to honor the custom. Abram did not demand it, that he loved Sarah there can be no doubt.

Sarai loved Abram. She called him lord. Her choice reads as a heartbreaking act of love.

God made a covenant with Abram and promised her husband that his seed would be blessed. Sarai had lived her life and marriage as the one who couldn't deliver in this area.

Could it be that she didn't doubt God's word to her husband, but that she doubted herself and value in God's eyes?

That she resigned herself to honor the law of the land, step aside and let her husband receive from someone else what she hadn't been able to give?

The surrogate mother was considered the woman's responsibility if she failed to produce an heir. Sarai chose Hagar as someone she trusted to be the healing for what society dictated to be her shame, and responsibility.

She took the idea of the handmaid to her husband and he agreed.

> *And Sarai said unto Abram, Behold now, the*
> *LORD hath restrained me from bearing: I pray*
> *thee, go in unto my maid; it may be that I may*
> *obtain children by her. And Abram hearkened to*
> *the voice of Sarai.*
> *Genesis 16:2*

> *And he went in unto Hagar, and she conceived: and*
> *when she saw that she had conceived, her mistress*
> *was despised in her eyes.*
> *Genesis 16:4*

The seed of despising bore fruit readily, telling it had long before been planted and nurtured. That Sarai bore scorn during her childless years, and that it led to her actions, there can be little doubt.

Thirteen years later, God speaks again to Abram and clarifies the matter.

> *And when Abram was ninety years old and nine,*
> *the LORD appeared to Abram, and said unto him,*
> *I am the Almighty God; walk before me, and be*
> *thou perfect.*
> *And I will make my covenant between me and thee,*
> *and will multiply thee exceedingly.*
> *And Abram fell on his face: and God talked with*
> *him, saying,*
> *As for me, behold, my covenant is with thee, and*
> *thou shalt be a father of many nations.*
> *Neither shall thy name any more be called Abram,*
> *but thy name shall be Abraham; for a father of*
> *many nations have I made thee.*
> *And I will make thee exceeding fruitful, and I will*
> *make nations of thee, and kings shall come out of*
> *thee.*
> *And I will establish my covenant between me and*
> *thee and thy seed after thee in their generations for*
> *an everlasting covenant, to be a God unto thee, and*
> *to thy seed after thee....*
> *And God said unto Abraham, As for Sarai thy wife,*
> *thou shalt not call her name Sarai, but Sarah shall*
> *her name be.*
> *And I will bless her, and give thee a son also of her:*

yea, I will bless her, and she shall be a mother of
nations; kings of people shall be of her.
Then Abraham fell upon his face, and laughed, and
said in his heart, Shall a child be born unto him
that is an hundred years old? and shall Sarah, that
is ninety years old, bear?
And Abraham said unto God, O that Ishmael
might live before thee!
And God said, Sarah thy wife shall bear thee a son
indeed; and thou shalt call his name Isaac: and I
will establish my covenant with him for an
everlasting covenant, and with his seed after him.
And as for Ishmael, I have heard thee: Behold, I
have blessed him, and will make him fruitful, and
will multiply him exceedingly; twelve princes shall
he beget, and I will make him a great nation.
But my covenant will I establish with Isaac, which
Sarah shall bear unto thee at this set time in the
next year.
Genesis 17:1-7, 15-21

The Lord establishes His covenant between Abraham and Sarah. Her name is changed along with Abraham's and a miracle is promised for her womb.

The Lord then returns shortly with witnesses and reaffirms the promise to bless Sarah. Notice her reaction mirrors her husbands but with different consequences.

And they said unto him, Where is Sarah thy wife?
And he said, Behold, in the tent.
And he said, I will certainly return unto thee
according to the time of life; and, lo, Sarah thy wife
shall have a son. And Sarah heard it in the tent
door, which was behind him.
Now Abraham and Sarah were old and well
stricken in age; and it ceased to be with Sarah after
the manner of women.
Therefore Sarah laughed within herself, saying,
After I am waxed old shall I have pleasure, my lord
being old also?
And the LORD said unto Abraham, Wherefore did
Sarah laugh, saying, Shall I of a surety bear a child,
which am old?

Is any thing too hard for the LORD? At the time
appointed I will return unto thee, according to the
time of life, and Sarah shall have a son.
Then Sarah denied, saying, I laughed not; for she
was afraid. And he said, Nay; but thou didst laugh.
Genesis 18:9-15

The Lord directs His word to her soul. He confronts the pain, the near self-derision, etched in through years of fiery trails and disappointment. She, stilled by his word and belief that indeed nothing was to hard for Him, is fearful.

God clearly lets her know, He hears her. He knows her. He considers her pain and promises to bless her.

She expresses the fear of the Lord, she reacts to His all knowing holiness. She believes Him.

When Sarah gives birth, she and Abraham name their son Isaac, which means laughter, marking the significance of the interaction.

And the LORD visited Sarah as he had said, and
the LORD did unto Sarah as he had spoken.
For Sarah conceived, and bare Abraham a son in
his old age, at the set time of which God had spoken
to him.
And Abraham called the name of his son that was
born unto him, whom Sarah bare to him, Isaac.
And Abraham circumcised his son Isaac being eight
days old, as God had commanded him.
And Abraham was an hundred years old, when his
son Isaac was born unto him.
And Sarah said, God hath made me to laugh, so
that all that hear will laugh with me.
And she said, Who would have said unto Abraham,
that Sarah should have given children suck? for I
have born him a son in his old age.
Genesis 21:1-7

The Lord blessed Sarah with joy. Through Sarah's womb and miracle child an everlasting covenant would come, Christ the Messiah.

Through faith also Sara herself received strength to
conceive seed, and was delivered of a child when she
was past age, because she judged him faithful who

had promised.
Hebrews 11:11

Prior to bringing judgment on Sodom and Gomorrah, God confronts the pain and fear in Sarah's heart and He promises her joy.

He knows the knocks we take in this life, our frailty, and all we must overcome. If we trust in Him and believe in reverence of His Holiness, His omnipotence, we live in and express the fear of the Lord.

The LORD taketh pleasure in them that fear him,
in those that hope in his mercy.
Psalm 147:11

As with wisdom's woman we see in beautiful Sarah the fear of the Lord. She trusts in Him and His word, she follows Him unwaveringly and through her all nations are blessed.

MODERN WORLD

The Gospel preached throughout the world.

"ALMOST 7 BILLION MOBILE-CELLULAR SUBSCRIPTIONS WORLDWIDE"

"The developing countries are home to more than three quarters of all mobile-cellular subscriptions..."

"The number of mobile-cellular subscriptions worldwide is approaching the number of people on earth. Mobile- cellular subscriptions will reach almost 7 billion by end 2014, corresponding to a penetration rate of 96%."

"ALMOST 3 BILLION PEOPLE — 40% OF THE WORLD'S POPULATION — ARE USING THE INTERNET"

"Close to one out of three people in the developing countries are online..."

"44% OF HOUSEHOLDS HAVE INTERNET ACCESS AT HOME"

"In Africa, only one out of ten households is connected."

ICT facts and figures 2014[22]

> *But thou, O Daniel, shut up the words, and seal the book, even to the time of the end: many shall run to and fro, and knowledge shall be increased.*
> *Daniel 12:4*

Worldwide communication is happening in our day. If 96% of the population can receive a text, we can consider the day is nigh.

TAKING IT TO HEART

*The secret of the LORD is with them that fear him;
and he will shew them his covenant.*
Psalms 25:14

*Behold, the eye of the LORD is upon them that fear
him, upon them that hope in his mercy;
To deliver their soul from death, and to keep them
alive in famine.*
Psalms 33:18,19

*Oh how great is thy goodness, which thou hast laid
up for them that fear thee; which thou hast wrought
for them that trust in thee before the sons of men!
Thou shalt hide them in the secret of thy presence
from the pride of man: thou shalt keep them secretly
in a pavilion from the strife of tongues.*
Psalms 31:19,20

*The angel of the LORD encampeth round about
them that fear him, and delivereth them.
O taste and see that the LORD is good: blessed is the
man that trusteth in him.*
Psalms 34:7,8

*For as the heaven is high above the earth, so great is
his mercy toward them that fear him.*
Psalms 103:11

PERSONAL APPLICATION

Knowing that the prophecies are being fulfilled, how should we prepare? Let's take a moment to prayerfully apply God's word to our lives.

FAITH

What can we do to build/protect our faith?

We can trust in the Lord, no matter how inadequate we may feel.

> *As soon as Jesus heard the word that was spoken, he saith unto the ruler of the synagogue, Be not afraid, only believe.*
> *Mark 5:36*

List ways you are inspired to believe, trust and walk in the fear of the Lord, in regard to your faith.

LOVE

What can we do to build/ protect our love?

Love our families, forgive our own and their frailties. Forgive the frailties of others. Trust in the Lord's love.

When moments of doubt of your worth cloud your mind and color your actions, just ask Him; Father, do you love me?

List ways you are inspired to believe, trust and walk in the fear of the Lord, in regard to your love and family.

HOME

What can we do to build/ protect our homes?

Food storage profits our families in these days of sorrows but it could also be available for others when things get much worse.

When the church is raptured, who might come to your home? Strangers? Only the Lord knows.

What testament of love can you leave for Christ Jesus? What will they need beside food and shelter?

Bibles, books on the tribulation and Revelations...

List ways you are inspired to believe, trust and walk in the fear of the Lord, in regard to your home and security.

Praise Him: He is so good, let Him know.

NOTES:

NOTES:

APPENDIX ONE

1. Two such men who have tenaciously gone after the truth and the validity of the Holy Bible are; Josh McDowell *Evidence That Demands a Verdict* ISBN: 0918956463, and Lee Strobel *A Case For Christ* ISBN: 0739441833 . Excellent resources for those inundated with disparaging remarks concerning the validity of God's word.

2. http://www.internationalrelations.com/wars-in-progress/

3. http://www.equatoriasun.com/latest-news/south-sudan-crisis-famine-and-genocide-threaten-to-engulf-nation/

4. http://www.unicef.org/drought/drought-countries.htm

4.1. http://www.mapreport.com/subtopics/d/0.html

4.2. http://earthquake.usgs.gov/earthquakes/index.php

5. http://www.fews.net/

6. http://www.reuters.com/article/2014/08/11/us-health-ebola-toll-idUSKBN0GB27Z20140811

7. http://thediplomat.com/2014/03/famine-threatens-pakistan/

8. http://www.cbn.com/cbnnews/us/2014/February/Facebook-Read-More-Than-the-Bible/

9. http://www.marketingcharts.com/online/social-networking-eats-up-3-hours-per-day-for-the-average-american-user-26049/

10. http://www.ipsos-na.com/news-polls/pressrelease.aspx?id=5954

10.1. http://www.bls.gov/tus/tables/a1_2013.pdf

11. http://www.project-syndicate.org/commentary/bernard-haykel-and-cole-bunzel-consider-the-implications-of-the-islamic-state-s-declaration-of-a-caliphate

12. http://www.worldwatchlist.us/

13. http://flashtrafficblog.wordpress.com/2014/08/07/jihadist-rampage-hamas-threatens-to-relaunch-war-isis-beheading-children-christians-in-iraq-170000-killed-in-syria/

13.1. http://flashtrafficblog.wordpress.com/2014/08/14/i-have-just-interviewed-an-iraqi-pastor-on-the-terrible-persecution-christians-in-iraq-are-facing-please-listen-share-with-others/

14. http://www.persecution.org/2014/04/26/christians-targeted-in-global-persecution/

15. http://aspe.hhs.gov/poverty/14poverty.cfm

16. http://web.stanford.edu/group/scspi/sotu/SOTU_2014_CPI.pdf

17. (Full report, slow link) http://www.frbsf.org/community-development/files/cp_fullreport.pdf

18. http://www.cbpp.org/cms/index.cfm?fa=view&id=3252

19. http://www.theguardian.com/society/2014/aug/07/antisemitism-rise-europe-worst-since-nazis

20. https://www.pcusa.org/resource/religious-demographic-profile-presbyterians-2011/

21. *Every Woman in the Bible*, By Sue and Larry Richards, ISBN: 0785214410.

22. http://www.itu.int/en/ITU-D/Statistics/Pages/facts/default.aspx

Additional: Websites for disaster preparedness:

http://www.redcross.org/prepare/location/home-family/get-kit

http://www.fema.gov/media-library/assets/documents/34326

http://www.fema.gov/media-library/assets/documents/90354

http://www.ready.gov/sites/default/files/documents/files/checklist_1.pdf

http://www.ready.gov/build-a-kit

http://emergency.cdc.gov/preparedness/kit/disasters/

http://emergency.cdc.gov/preparedness/kit/water/index.asp

http://emergency.cdc.gov/preparedness/kit/food/index.asp

APPENDIX TWO

Chapter One

Home canning and drying foods:

A food dehydrator is an excellent investment, making the most of seasonal fruits and vegetables with minimal need for storage space. A large box of tomatoes or strawberries can be condensed down to the space of a few large mason jars.

If you do not own a food dehydrator you can still easily dry foods in your oven. Slice thin place on baking sheets oven 120-140 F.

The University of Colorado has an exceptional resource chart available online, plus here are a few others:

http://www.ext.colostate.edu/pubs/foodnut/09309.html

http://www.rrc.ksu.edu/p.aspx?tabid=30

http://nchfp.uga.edu/how/dry.html

In this economy canning your own jams and jellies is definitely wise, and the flavor will spoil you for store bought jam. If you have never tried making jam, it is a creatively satisfying endeavor.

NOTES:

Chapter Two

Store bought staples high in protein:

Canned chicken, tuna, and salmon

Canned corned or chipped beef

Canned beans, refried beans, chili's

Peanut butter, nut butters, nuts

Dehydrated meats, beef jerky, soy

Pinto beans, navy beans, garbanzos

Favorite bulk beans, etc.

NOTES:

Chapter Three

Grains, cereals, pastas

Wheat, flour, cream of wheat

Oats, corn, rice

Lentils, barley, dried peas and chickpeas

Beans, pinto, red, navy and black beans

Oatmeal, cornmeal, grits

Baking mixes, baking soda and powder

Salt, yeast, Sourdough Starter, etc.

NOTES:

Chapter Four

Fruits:

Dried fruits

Raisins, cranberries, cherries

Banana chips, fruit leather etc.

Canned fruits, juices, applesauce

Vegetables:

Dried Vegetables

Potatoes, onions, cabbage

Tomatoes, carrots etc.

Canned vegetables, juices, sauces

NOTES:

Chapter Five

Quick meals for times of duress.

Meals: Readymade Emergency=Soup mixes made in jars.

Military MREs (Meal Ready to Eat) emergency food packets are expensive and daunting to the average woman. In times of duress however the logic is; the easier the better. The ideal emergency meal would be nutritious and cost effective.

We can make our own economical, nutritious emergency meals. Although not ready to eat out of packet, ours are instant, just add water. They are your basic Christmas soup mix in a mason jar, often delivered by your sweet neighbor or friend.

Just pack them in storage bags, label with instructions, and store in an out of the way container. A large popcorn tin works well.

Remember ones that call for beans that need to be soaked will just add intestinal duress to already present stress if not soaked and rinsed properly. For emergency time savers look for recipes made with rice, lentils, barley, pasta, and dried or instant potatoes.

It seems everyone has at least one favorite to share. They can be readily found online, in recipe and Christmas gift books. Here is a standard adapted recipe to get you started.

Wild Rice & Barley Soup

Grains (pint size bag)

1/2 cup wild rice

1/2 cup barley

Season mix (mix, place in separate snack size bag)

1/4 cup dried minced onion

1/4 cup beef bouillon granules

2 Tbsp. dried shredded carrots

1 Tbsp. brown sugar

1 tsp. dried basil

1 tsp. dried oregano

1 tsp. dried parsley

1/2 tsp. pepper

1/2 tsp. dried garlic or garlic powder

1/4 tsp. dried celery or celery powder

Optional

Dried mushrooms slices or additional dried vegetables of your choice.

Add season bag to pint size grains bag, seal and label with instructions, (these can be written on with permanent marker): Add to 7 cups of water, bring to boil then simmer approx. 1 hour, serves 6.

Find soups and adjust seasons and bouillons to your families taste. They are also handy on a cold winters day, or a busy one.

NOTES:

NOTES:

Chapter Six

For the pantry:

A list of numbers/times/places of community services in your area.

If you don't already know, find out the times and distributions of bread lines, breadbaskets and commodities where you live. Find out which ones give clothes away for free.

These number/times/places can be discreetly passed on to those in need, or available to pass on to a friend who needs the information. Consider giving to these charities. You can discretely drop donations off after service times, and they need our generosity.

These places are where the hardest hit souls will be, who have the most need, and little enough money for housing let alone to spend at a thrift store.

NOTES:

Chapter Seven

Recommended water:

At least a three-day supply of water per person.

1 gallon per person per day.

Two quarts for drinking and two quarts for each person in your household for food preparation/sanitation.

Safety instructions for questionable water:

Boiling, full boil at least 1 minute/up to 10 minutes, 149 degrees Fahrenheit.

Bleach containing no additives, 1/8 tsp. per gallon for clear water, 1/4 tsp. per gallon for cloudy water.

Food storage basics:

Liquid meals, shakes, protein drinks

Herbal teas, instant coffee, drink mixes

Powdered milk, powdered creamer, hot cocoa mix

Concentrated canned juices, milk, etc.

NOTES:

Chapter Eight

Specialty and necessity Items:

Spices, seasonings, herbs

Oils, olive oil, vegetable oil

Sugar, honey, sweeteners

Syrups, chocolate, hard candies

Trail mix, granola cereal and protein bars

Instant foods, soups, stews

Crackers, cookies, popcorn etc.

NOTES:

Chapter Nine

Other emergency necessities:

Maintenance supplies and other necessities:

Tools, paper and toiletry supplies,

Means of safety and security,

Batteries, charger, radio

Matches/lighter, lanterns, flashlight

Camp stove cookery or hibachi, candles

Safety pins, duct tape, tarps

First-aid kit with antihistamine and aspirin and other needed medications, etc.

NOTES:

About the Author

D. A. Fiedler is an American writer and author of the novel, *Alabaster*.

Made in the USA
Middletown, DE
31 July 2015